THE ROMANCE
OF PREACHING

JAMES W. ANGELL

D1710928

CSS Publishing Company, Inc.
Lima, Ohio

THE ROMANCE OF PREACHING

Scripture quotations marked (KJV) are from the *King James Version of the Bible*,
in the public domain.

Scripture quotations marked (NRSV) are from the *New Revised Standard Version
of the Bible,* copyright 1989, by the Division of Christian Education of the National
Council of the Churches of Christ in the USA. Used by permission.

Scripture quotations marked (RSV) are from the *Revised Standard Version of the
Bible,* copyrighted 1946, 1952 (c), 1971, 1973, by the Division of Christian Education of the National Council of the Churches of Christ in the USA. Used by permission.

Library of Congress Cataloging-in-Publication Data

Angell, James W.
    The romance of preaching / James W. Angell.
      p.   cm.
    ISBN 0-7880-0574-X
    1. Preaching. 2. Angell, James W. I. Title.
BV4211.2.A46 1995
251—dc20   95-13429
                                             CIP

"What Tomas Said in a Pub" by James Stephens from *Collected Poems,* copyright
(c) 1931 by Macmillan and Co., Ltd. Used by permission of The Society of Authors,
London, on behalf of the copyright owner, Mrs. Iris Wise.

Excerpt reprinted from *Minister's Prayer Book* by John Doberstein, copyright (c)
1958 Muhlenberg Press. Used by permission of Augsburg Fortress Publishers.

Excerpt reprinted from *This People, This Parish* by Robert K. Hudnut, copyright
(c) 1986 Zondervan Publishing. Used by permission of the author.

ISBN 0-7880-0574-X   PRINTED IN U.S.A.

With gratitude, for the people of

First Presbyterian Church
Indianola, Iowa

Second Presbyterian Church
Lexington, Kentucky

Westwood Presbyterian Church
Los Angeles, California

Claremont Presbyterian Church
Claremont, California

The Presbyterian Church of Westfield
Westfield, New Jersey

St. Mark Presbyterian Church
Newport Beach, California

Madison Avenue Presbyterian Church
New York, New York

Other Books By James W. Angell

Open Your Heart to Spring

The Gospel in Glass

Put Your Arms Around the City

When God Made You, He Knew What He Was Doing

Dare to Hope

O Susan!

How to Spell Presbyterian

Seek It Lovingly

Slice Me a Piece of Summer

Roots and Wings

Learning to Manage Our Fears

Accept No Imitations

The Gift Book

Table Of Contents

Preface

"I've got another book in my head," he said, putting aside the completed manuscript that told the story of his first year with cancer. "It's about preaching, about my love for preaching. I think I could sketch out the chapter titles."

It was the autumn of 1992, three months before Dad died. Since returning from New York where Dad was the interim minister at Madison Avenue Presbyterian Church, he and mother had been living in their lovely home in the foothills above Claremont, California, with a sweeping view of the Inland Valley below. He was spending most of his time on the couch, too weak to type or sit for long at his desk. Clearly he was living on borrowed time. Nevertheless, I encouraged him to begin this book. Before my visit ended a week later, not only had he scratched out the chapter titles on his familiar yellow legal pad, but he had also drafted two chapters, which I took back home to Houston to start typing. Over the next six weeks Dad continued to develop the other chapters, sometimes able to write in his own hand and sometimes dictating to my mother. He invited a fellow writer up to the house for a couple of sessions to discuss the right approach. I typed up new material as soon as Mom sent it, visited again to discuss revisions, and by mid-November we had a first draft of this book. Dad died before Christmas.

As I look back now at those first handwritten pages, I remember what joy he found in writing about his career and what force of will he exercised to see this project through. With his life rushing toward an end, he was determined to leave this gift — an account of his love affair with preaching.

I was four years old when Dad left a budding law career to enter theological seminary. Throughout my childhood and teen years I witnessed his career as a Presbyterian minister take

7

flight, hardly knowing what to make of the multiple roles he had. Every Sunday he presided over worship, prayed, and preached; and I knew by people's faces that his sermons inspired them. He answered the telephone at all hours of the day and night, talking in tones of comfort and concern; he visited hospitals and homes; he attended countless night meetings, just as often in the larger community as at the church, especially during the years of the civil rights movement. He traveled to meetings of Presbytery and Synod; he served on the boards of universities and orphanages; he played the Christ in a city-wide Easter pageant several successive years; he published a collection of sermons and then began writing books.

There was no part of Dad's job as a minister that he disliked or wished otherwise; each role seemed to be flush with meaning and purpose for him. But it was the preparation of the sermon that framed his weekly schedule, and it was the act of preaching that focused his energy, bringing him closest to the fulfillment of his calling.

Dad would often say that a congregation makes a preacher. He was pastor to seven congregations during his career, and he believed that each congregation challenged him to further develop his powers in the pulpit. I think that he would dedicate this book to the congregations who loved him and inspired him to realize his ideal of useful and imaginative preaching.

Ann V. Angell
Atlanta, Georgia
November 1994

Foreword

I was at my desk working on the next deadline when the phone rang. "This is Jim Angell," the voice said. "I'm trying to put together a book on preaching, and I wonder whether you could come up and talk about it."

Jim was dying of cancer, and his call was a surprise. Two days before, I had phoned his wife Virginia to see whether I could pay him a visit. She had said it was not a good day. So I sent him a card with a drawing of a hard riding cowboy, inscribing it, "This is Jim, headin' for the last round-up." I had figured I would not see him again this side of the river.

It took me no time to reach his living room. He told me that after more than 40 years in the ministry, he wanted to record some thoughts and experiences that might be helpful to younger preachers. He said he had read things I had written, and thought I might be of help in pulling some of his material together.

It was indeed flattering to be asked for assistance by one of America's premier preachers, the kind of platform communicator one can truly call a "prince of the pulpit." So to say I took his request seriously would be an understatement. It was obvious he did not have long to work on the piece himself.

Although I was by no means an intimate of James W. Angell, we were not strangers. The first time I saw him was in 1969 at his installation as senior pastor of the Claremont Presbyterian Church, which he was to serve for 18 years until his retirement in 1987. (His popular book *How to Spell Presbyterian* is still widely used in confirmation classes.) I was a follower of his "Answer" column in *A.D.* magazine, published a few years ago jointly by the Presbyterians and the United Church of Christ.

9

Jim had told me that my uncle M. Willard Lampe, who was dean of the School of Religion at the University of Iowa when Jim was a law student there, was helpful when he was choosing between law and the ministry. My cousin the Rev. John A. Lampe baptized the Angells' daughter Susan in Chicago, when Jim was a student assistant from McCormick Theological Seminary at John's church in Rogers Park.

For a working title for the book, Jim was using "It Was A Fine Romance," an illusion to a popular Fred Astaire song. This was typical Angell. He drew some of his best themes from secular drama. But he agreed that in a book directed to a professional interest, it might be helpful if the title gave a clue to the content. Hence *The Romance Of Preaching*.

You could hardly say that Jim Angell welcomed death. Indeed he fought it with everything he had. During his last year, he made the 35-mile trip from Claremont into Los Angeles every Monday for intensive sessions at the Norris Cancer Treatment Center.

What he bought with all this effort was a productive and satisfying final year. It saw at least two books written, including this one, community talks and inspiring guest sermons, the marriage of a daughter, and his and Virginia's 50th wedding anniversary. When the end came, he was ready. He went out with style.

It was, to be sure, a fine romance.

T. Willard Hunter
Claremont, California
February 1995

Author's Note

For whom is this book intended?

When I began, I hoped someone was ready to listen to what I was eager to say. After 42 years as a minister, I still was not always sure. But I never stopped believing I had the best job in the world.

Maybe this is for Max, who is in his final year in seminary. After a year of service to the people of Guatemala, he is ready to combine that kind of ministry with another.

Or perhaps for the dozen or more ministers — like Karen or Steven, or Tom, "Bear," or Rob — younger colleagues in whose lives and work I have taken pride over the past few years.

There may be others. As everyone with a love for the church and a connection with the preaching and pastoral ministry knows, much of the romance has disappeared. A good deal of it has been lost in a fog of bureaucratic preoccupation, or has perished on the hot, hard pavement of indifference. Sam Shoemaker, who walked tall among leaders of the church generations ago, once put it in the form of a question: "Where goes the glow?"

Maybe this book will fall into the hands of a few who are trying to decide whether the ministry is right for them. Rather than science, law, teaching, or medicine. I hope so.

I have never been a homiletics teacher, though I had some very good ones myself. I have some fear of underqualification, since the lapse of four decades may have left my skills too much bound up with yesterday.

If I am unsure of that, what I am terribly sure about is my love for the job, a true sense of call, and an eagerness to combine all the gifts of creativity we know anything about with the summons to be messengers of good news, interpreters of a mystery greater than the placement of the stars — the mystery we know as the incarnation.

And if the early preaching principles that provided me with my first formal guidance change — or if they take on a sense of datedness — the truth for which we have been called to be responsible stewards does not.

Preaching is, and should be, hard work. It is not light entertainment. It is part of the energy of justice. It is a pain shared. It is moral leadership. It means taking positions that may prove unpopular. It is one of the answers to our search for personal completeness. It is compassion and hope, childhood and age, being born and saying good-bye to life, and helping people know both God and themselves. Preaching is as essential as farming — as important to a safe and decent future for humankind as a sixth grade class taught by a trained teacher or a cure for a deadly disease.

If this small addition to the literature of the pulpit either initiates or restores the romance of the call to preach, I will call the effort worthwhile.

James W. Angell
Claremont, California
1992

Chapter 1

To Search The Heart With Candles, And A Man Named Angell James

I was ten when I first got an inkling that someday I might wind up as a preacher. Our Iowa newspaper carried Ripley's "Believe It Or Not" as a daily feature in a lower corner of the comic page. And, to my considerable amazement, one night I found there "Arch Angell," my father's name. I knew the family name "Angell" usually seemed good for a smile, but putting "Arch" with "Angell" hadn't seemed to me uproariously odd or funny.

Angels, I would learn, are agents of God — servants, voices, warriors, desert ministers, champions of righteousness. And, if Dad enjoyed that kind of rank, maybe there was a place for me too in looking after heaven's business, even though there were no other family clergy to use as models.

The call eventually would come, and yes, I would, in time, set my face in a direction that would supply my next 40 years of life with ineffable beauty and sense of purpose. Along the road I would also make a fascinating discovery: that 150 years before, at the famous Carr's Lane Church in Birmingham, England, there was a pastor who would help me understand who I wanted to be, and what I wanted to be like.

His name — scarcely believable in the light of this total story — was Angell James. His profound influence at Carr's Lane, including his collected sermons, are a legacy that in later years inspired me to sit down and write how the pulpit has managed to become so passionately precious to me.

Pulpits, like ministers who stand behind them, come in all shapes and sizes. Some pulpits are no more than desks with fluorescent lights. Others resemble thrones. In cathedrals they may look like gazebos suspended from a wall, draped in paraments that reflect seasons of the church year. In simpler places of worship, a pulpit may hold a Bible. Another may resemble a holy box, adorned with carvings of fish, or the disciples.

In the Scottish Kirk, pulpits are often accessible only by climbing a few steps with a door to be closed by the preacher after entering. A Glasgow lad, it is said, having witnessed one of those dramatic door closings, became anxious when the preacher launched into the sermon with flailing arms. Tugging at his mother's sleeve, he whispered, "What will we do if he gets out of there?"

Today's pulpits are frequently occupied by women. Hurrah for that!

In remote parishes they often stand empty as prairie winds blow across wide fields managed by absentee owners. The people are gone. Pulpits may be found in hospitals, prison, or school chapels, on cruise ships, or as a piece of equipment used annually for baccalaureates.

It took the Reformation to shift the pulpit to the forefront. The Table had always been the main focus of divine activity. In apostolic times a boat or a bench in the synagogue would do.

This book is about the pulpit and those who find it an irresistible part of their being, a romantic place, a scary place, yet where the mystery of the incarnation continues to unfold like a story with chapters still being written. It is not about technique. Rather it is about how those who walk into the pulpit and utter that amazing formula, "listen for the Word of God," can better live up to the significance they represent.

Television and the long recreational weekend have made the pulpit increasingly less useful in defining what life is about or for. Income is more important. A good education gets you started up the ladder. Fitness helps you sustain your momentum. Computers, home entertainment centers, fashionable friends round out the middle class menu. To listen to preaching

14

and to try to fathom its connection with the struggle for meaning and happiness may rank barely above the newspaper's horoscope and just slightly below tomorrow's appointment with the dentist.

Life, though, is more than ownership and dramas of distraction, brought in by cable. It is urgent, precious, tentative, fragile. Beautiful as roses. It is courage, growth, forgiveness, and love. Confronting two realities — our human mortality, and the omnipresence of goodness in an imperfect world. It is God trying to break through, and people who have learned to listen to each other. It is laughter and silence — it is not getting lost. Grief. Adventure. Second chances and celebration.

In a word, poetry.

In New Zealand there's a range of mountains named The Remarkables. From a hotel balcony in Queenstown, they look like the divine signature scrawled.

We've lived, and continue to live through remarkable times. And that's what preaching is about, too, as one hunk of history interfaces with another, and we face the wonder of knowing how uniquely splendid our common life actually is.

When the record is sealed on the present fabulous century, it will go down as a time of record-breaking discoveries. The expiring century will include the usual wars and depressions. But along with appalling genocides, there were footsteps on the moon. Miracles beyond counting, the beginnings of a system of world government, atomic fission, a super-collider in Texas, a computer center as big as five football fields in New York. It will be remembered for organ transplants, bullet trains, and super-highways — an 18-year increase in life expectancy for most since the century began.

And we continue to be searchers. Craving acceptance and hints as to where we fit into the plan if there is one. We pursue recognition, pleasure, meaning, God.

We use our telescopes to map the skies, investigate the architecture of the molecule, hold a million seminars. Yet come away unsatisfied — though increasingly sure that we are souls rather than statistics. That, even if we can't put it in comprehensible terms, we belong to something eternal. We wear and bear the *imago dei*, the image of God.

One of the priorities of preaching is to maintain guard over this way of understanding existence. The brush of angel wings. Confidence that we are in possession of at least a couple of clues as to why the universe is here.

A long time ago a prophet named Zephaniah heard some words from heaven and passed them on. He heard God saying: "I will search Jerusalem with candles, and punish those who are stagnant in spirit" (KJV 1:12).

If we are searchers, then so is the One who has breathed into our being upon whatever it is that death cannot touch. God is also looking for something from us. And when our gazes meet, it's Big Bang all over again.

Today candles are either brought into use when power supplies are interrupted or when we try to add magic touches to an otherwise ordinary evening. Once they were as essential as bread. Now they herald protest marches and glamorize the sanctuary at weddings or on Christmas Eve.

A hundred and fifty years ago the pastor of Carr's Lane church in Birmingham sat down to write to a troubled parishioner, with Zephaniah's words brooding in his brain, for here is what he wrote: "If you will search your heart with candles, you will find the help you seek."

When I discovered that sentence in a *Collection of the Life and Letters of John A. James*, the text cast a fresh glow upon my sense of what the gospel is about, just as it must have eased the heart of the one who got the letter.

To seek for God *within* is, of course, not the whole course of study. The "God within" no more exhausts the full meaning of God than the God of sky or the God of history.

But to look within and find only emptiness may suggest something about the problem of our times as much as the search for solutions to a healthy economy, or how to rescue the environment.

In an age that tries to keep justice high on its agenda, discussions about the inward journey may sound like we're on the wrong page.

But that is not accurate if the quest is honest. It does not deny community, and moves us continually closer both to God and to the main purpose of our lives. God's promise "to search Jerusalem with candles" may be a reference to discipline because it is followed by a threat of punishment to those who abandon the task of finding out who they are, who allow themselves to become "stagnant in spirit." More about that later.

I have the feeling, however, that when Angell James used the words from the Zephaniah text to help a church member find his way through a hard time, he found in those words something better than a warning.

He also recognized in a candle-bearer a Presence, the ultimate acolyte to our pain, the Morning Star of all our dreams.

Which is what makes preaching both useful and sublime, and as essential to our future as repairing the nation's infrastructure, or keeping the weak safe and the strong generous.

Preaching has been the crowning fulfillment of my life. It affords the most intimate form of a conversation between persons this side of Lover's Lane.

The preacher's search is actually the victory of everyone.

Phillips Brooks called preaching "truth through personality." But beyond the definitions is the fire that has to burn away the dross and help us to see that our lives genuinely matter, that there are things that moth and rust cannot corrupt. And the church is the candle shop with fragrances that keep bringing us back for more.

For solutions to those feuds and prejudices that poison the water and make it bitter.

For visions brave enough to help us start to bring about a planetary salvation.

I'll try to trace my own journeys, one of which will lead us into a strange, wonderful world we call Eastern Kentucky — where hillsides are still plowed by mules, and where children still have to cross the Big Sandy on swinging bridges to reach home after school.

In one of these Appalachian "coal camps" I found myself one day with an invitation to ride a moving belt on my stomach into the center of the mine where explosives were in the process of being set off, and the shattered seams were then loaded into little iron-wheeled cars to be transported to waiting trucks outside.

That day I wore, as all miners do, a cap with a light on it.

Preachers are like that. Even if they make no other contribution, the ones who are convinced that the Spirit both speaks and acts through them defy the darkness of the mountain and say to all who will listen, "Watch and I will show you the Light of life."

That is what I learned from Angell James.

Chapter 2

After A Lost Election, Field Of Dreams

Iowa is an Indian word meaning "beautiful land." And that's where it all began for me.

I started out on a legal career and passed the Iowa bar. Long before, though, I had harbored thoughts of one day becoming a preacher. Sunday school had not been a bore as it often is for many kids. Attending summer youth conferences, then Bible classes in college — taught by Dr. Howard Legg, who looked like he belonged in the Senate rather than in a college classroom — set the stage for an invitation one August to give the sermon in my home church. I was 20. From that day on I was hooked — at least in my private thoughts — though it would be a whole war later before I would have enough confidence and courage to set those first plans aside and begin seminary.

Iowa was a good place to be born. A beautiful land indeed. Rolling green hills, small towns, extreme weather. The only "gang" we heard about worked on the railroad. In summer, the sky was robin-egg blue. Christmases were most often cold and white, just like the song.

Kevin Costner's *Field Of Dreams* is in the eastern part of the state. My birthplace was in western Iowa, a town called Atlantic, located just 40 miles from the border-defining Missouri River. But dreams were abundant for my generation — at bargain prices.

I grew up in the presence of good books, Grace Barnard's smile at the bank, football practice, declamatory contests, working-class parents determined that I would have opportunities that had been denied them.

19

In 1947, I went back to Atlantic to practice law.

I had graduated with honors from the University of Iowa Law School, passed the bar, the War Years were over, and now an excellent opportunity had opened up for me to practice in the legal profession among people I had known and lived with all my life.

A prominent law firm by the name of Boorman and Whitmore had invited me, because of the death of Mr. Boorman, to ply my trade there as a young attorney.

Other lawyers in the town also welcomed me, and my life seemed off to a successful start — though a combination of things, my upbringing, an intellectual pilgrimage that had caught fire in college, plus three and a half years at sea, had left me with the nagging thought that maybe the ministry, rather than law, was where I belonged.

One day Mr. Whitmore called me into his office with a flattering suggestion.

"Jim," he said, "if it's okay with you, I'd like to nominate you for City Attorney. You haven't had a lot of experience, but I know you can do it. May I have your permission to make the nomination?"

"Of course," I said. How could I say no to that?

Another lawyer in town with much more experience was also being proposed for the job. Roscoe Jones was a good and long-time friend of my father and mother, and someone who also had been most friendly to me — and honestly so.

The night the city council met, the vote was 3 for Mr. Jones and 3 for me. The mayor had to cast the deciding vote, and he voted for Jones.

I wasn't shattered by that turn of events. I would have been surprised to have been chosen, given my very junior qualifications. But I remember walking home from the council chamber that night with a new lightness of spirit, with some feelings of freedom that seemed to say, "If you're determined to go to Seminary, you can still go. The light has just gone green."

I was ordained on a February night in 1950, after it had snowed most of the afternoon. Many of the highways that surrounded the little square-towered red brick church were closed. When I rose from my knees that night, after having made my vows, I knew, though, that it was the most right thing I had ever done.

My initial "call" was to the Presbyterian congregation in Indianola, Iowa, where I had gone to Simpson College. In that church I would be nurtured and equipped for a church career that would continue 42 years.

The newly-ordained minister asks, "Will I get a chance to do what I have been trained to do?" "Where" is a matter of keen interest — though "where" turns out to be one of the least important questions of all. A wise parishioner once told me, "It isn't *where* you are, but *what* you are."

And lucky is the pastor who does not begin as someone else's assistant, but who from the starting gate is faced with regular preaching opportunities, and must accept responsibility for both failures and successes. Perhaps most important is the privilege of standing close to people in their sorrows, joys, and general need of God.

I remained with that flock in Indianola slightly less than five years. Leaving them broke my heart, for these were people who had given me everything every young pastor needs. Looking back, I can still see those many wonderful faces, and relive most, if not all, of those shining moments that would help to light the path ahead.

A few days before that departure (by now we were husband, wife, and three children) I stumbled onto these words in John Doberstein's *Ministers' Prayer Book,* words I have reread many times since — written by the father of a young clergyman at the beginning of a pastorate:

> *I beg you, do not look upon Dortmund as a stepping-stone, but rather say: "Here I shall stay as long as it pleases God; if it be his will, until I die." Look upon every child, your confirmands, every member of the congregation as if you will have to give account for every soul on the day of the Lord Jesus. Every day commit all*

21

these human souls from the worst and weakest of hands,
namely your own, into the best and strongest of hands.
Then you will be able to carry on your ministry not only
without care but also with joy overflowing and joyful
hope.

— Friedreich von Bodelschwingh

There are many among my best memories of that first parish.

In a church school class the Bible reading was the story of the Good Samaritan, and about the priest and Levite who, prior to the Samaritan's arrival, "passed by on the other side." After listening to this violation of the laws of mercy, six-year-old Terry exclaimed, "Boy, Mr. Angell wouldn't do anything like that!" Let's hope he was right.

The stained glass windows, extraordinarily appealing from behind the pulpit during the organ prelude, left their mark upon my soul. And when the lower panes were tilted open on hot mornings, a bird would sometimes fly in and soar about, providing considerable competition for people's attention.

A youngster perished in a fire only a block from the manse. I remember the late night fire sirens, the family's pain, the cemetery's deep cold a few mornings later — how the service book shook in my hands, how I struggled to keep my voice firm and comforting, as my chin quivered in the freezing wind.

During that year, as the new young pastor, I came down with the mumps, just as Holy Week was beginning. It seemed like an awful disaster to me. The congregation took it in stride.

One day in the spring was designated Rose Sunday. And members were invited to choose a single rose from their gardens to be displayed at worship. Lee Beymer brought his Peace rose.

Weddings, ice-skating nights, remodeling the manse. Calling in a home where a middle-aged woman lay terminally ill and was being cared for by her mother. Agnes, the mother, made milkshakes and served all three of us, along with some cookies. That afternoon I saw the Holy Grail.

My next pastorate was in Lexington, Kentucky, where I followed a distinguished man of wisdom and experience. At age 69, Jesse Herrmann had suffered a fatal heart attack at the All-Star baseball game. That was in July.

By January I was ready to assume the role, though I was but half his age. My greatest asset: a young family easy for all to fall in love with.

Kentucky is Henry Clay, tobacco, thoroughbreds, whiskey — fields with grass that looks bluish when the winds of March and April blow across it. It's where county roads have names like Ironworks Pike, where horse farms are called Calumet, Coldstream, or Spendthrift. One Derby Day the clerk of session and I placed a bet on a horse named "Divine Comedy." He ran eighth.

It is tradition, affection — more varieties of beauty than the heart can remember. And for the next 12 years, Lexington became a place we still look back on with lump-in-the-throat appreciation. The sanctuary was Gothic. And to preach there, facing a great Transfiguration window on a Sunday morning was like having a reserved seat in heaven.

Jane Offutt lived on North Broadway in a handsome three-story made of native limestone. Her husband had been a physician. After his death, she now lived there alone, assisted by a devoted black man named Holly. Jane taught Sunday school and liked to tell this one on herself. On a Saturday night she had studied the next day's lesson especially hard and Sunday morning shared with her juniors the harvest of her scholarship. After a serious 15-minute introduction she asked if there were any questions. Pause. John, his fist tucked under his chin, then inquired: "Mrs. Offutt, have your two front teeth always been that far apart?"

The aristocratic small city dealt with changes brought about by the Civil Rights movement with courageous openness. The "colored" and "whites" signs came down. Black students moved into the dorms at the University of Kentucky. Second Church became recognized as having one of the clearest voices of all, appealing for the dismantling of segregation. Hubert Humphrey telephoned from the Senate Office Building to commend the town's progress toward helping to create a genuinely inclusive society.

I played the Christus in a city-wide Easter pageant that brought thousands of people early to the Coliseum. One summer as part of an international exchange, a minister in Wakefield, England, and I traded houses, cars and jobs. I became the Vicar of Wakefield, while the Wakefield pastor became an American for a season.

Fifty miles to the east just outside Berea, Appalachia begins. Here is coal country. Strangers are suspect. But loyalties, once established, are as fixed as the hills. Fascinating names of eastern Kentucky's hamlet world include Pippa Passes, Kingdom Come, Thousand Sticks, Cranks, and Crummies.

Bruce Davis liked to say he was the "senior elder." And he was. He also claimed that, after finishing the work of creation, God had made Kentucky, and used it as a signature for the final masterpiece. Learning that he was ill, I made a visit one day to his upstairs bedroom. I had left word at the church where I might be located in case I was needed. In the middle of talking with Bruce, the telephone rang. It was the hospital, asking me to come as soon as possible because of an emergency. I rose to leave, but he ordered me to "sit down." "There's an emergency here, too," he said. We talked and prayed some more. In a short while, he died.

Then, California — a name no longer as golden as it was in 1945, but where desert, ocean, and mountains are still fertilized by genius and creativity, making it one of the Seven Wonders of the modern world.

At the ripe age of 45, I heeded the Horace Greeley advice, and moved our family West in response to an invitation to become pastor of a fascinating congregation in West Los Angeles, near the University of California at Los Angeles (UCLA).

It still seemed like the New Frontier, though controversy over involvement in Viet Nam kept the city in a mild uproar much of the time. By now one of the Angell daughters was married and living in Georgia. But the rest of us yielded to this strange call of the western wild, forsaking the gentle ways of Kentucky for a new position where the pastor's study was only about 100 yards from the gravesite of Marilyn Monroe.

The first year was a time of adjustment, but we stayed with it. The Golden State has been, now, the anchor of our existence for more than a quarter of a century — long enough to have piled up more armfuls of adventures. California brought the beginning of a writing career, television appearances, and a national church leadership race. In 1974 I was nominated for the position of Moderator of the Presbyterian Church in the USA. The General Assembly, which gathers annually to decide these things, met that year in Louisville. On the Sunday morning when I departed from Los Angeles for the assembly, I received a friendly ride atop the shoulders of supporters. But in Louisville, I lost.

Despite the excitement of new horizons, the highest adventure for me was being preacher and pastor. The second California congregation that was "ours" for a time was in the college town of Claremont, east of Los Angeles. Preaching there was made doubly challenging when the sermon listeners included not a few professors and other academics. During my 18 years at Claremont Presbyterian Church, I supervised the groundbreaking for four new buildings. I helped establish an exchange program with the local Hebrew Temple, made trips with church elders to the Chino prison, and witnessed singers and dancers lift spirits on the wings of ecstasy. I learned countless things from talented staff, prayed with the people, and loved them. The benedictions of a long pastorate are many.

In Claremont there was an adventure in darkness, when our 21-year-old Susan was killed in a falling-asleep-at-the-wheel accident returning Easter Eve from a short holiday at the Grand Canyon. A call from the Highway Patrol at 5 a.m. on Easter morning changed life for us forever. Out of that darkness came my book *O Susan!*, which seems to have spoken to the hearts of many.

When "retirement age" arrived, instead of stopping work that I so much enjoyed, I undertook a series of short-term interim pastorates. Westfield, New Jersey, Newport Beach (back to California again). Then to New York City.

25

Living in the East meant more stretching, and checking up on our knowledge of American history.

The New Jersey church had been organized in 1728. On the edge of the Watchung Mountains, it had a Revolutionary War cemetery across the street, a picturesque adjoining lake, and a tall white steeple overlooking the town of Westfield, the symbol of things everlasting. The ambience of the Seaboard is a mellow mix of Harvard and Yale, West Point, Fifth Avenue, Wall Street, Vermont, Gettysburg, Brooklyn, Harlem, the Delaware and Hudson rivers. As different from California as Long Island Sound is from the Mojave desert.

Being part of the teeming city of New York was different from being a visitor. It was a good feeling to sense that some of it was mine — that, for a little while, I was one with its energy, its diversity, museums, libraries, concert halls, subway trains, and historic memories and bustling harbor. That 18-month stay changed me in some ways that I like. The Madison Avenue Presbyterian Church had had but three pastors during the major portion of the twentieth century — all household names in the world of the church: Henry Sloan Coffin, George Arthur Buttrick, and David H. C. Read.

But to be a New Yorker is and always has been, to identify with the plight of strangers (bus drivers are often amazingly kind), with the dispossessed, with the grandeur of Central Park, and with the best of nearly everything.

Would I want to repeat these past 40 years — so filled as they have been with overflowing inspiration, variety, and stretching?

Yes. Yes — again and again. Wherever we went there were children in search of visions and people in search of affirmation. Grief, steadfastness of soul, a yearning for the balm of Gilead. Laughter and picnics. Supper of Bread and Wine. The Book. The community which, when we make it our own, transforms the world and what we come to expect of it.

Chapter 3

Preaching Because We Have Something To Say Rather Than Because We Have To Say Something

The pulpit is less than half of the mystery of preaching. If we attempt to separate it from what is happening on the listening side, it can be an empty gong or a clanging cymbal. Sermons are one-dimensional until a warming current begins to flow along the fragile wiring of the heart.

One Sunday at 10:55 a.m. I was stopped in the hallway by a young church member who appeared in great distress. He asked me, as the preacher who would be leading the service, if it would be all right if I asked the congregation to remain a few minutes after the benediction so he might speak to them. His request unnerved me a little. I had no idea what it was he wanted to say. There were only two minutes left before the chimes would ring and start the Introit and Call to Worship. But this was obviously most important. I asked him more about his request.

The day before, while driving along the Main Street of nearby Mt. Sterling, he had experienced a Grand Mal seizure that caused him to lose control of the car. It left the traffic lane, jumped the curb, and plunged through the door of a bank. While no one was hurt or killed, this discovery about a serious problem of which he had had no previous knowledge — and the threat it posed to both his job and the security of his family — had left him in a state of near terror. He would ask the members to pray for him. The chimes had now finished the ringing. The opening words of the service would have to await the tardy minister.

"Let me think about it," I said. "I will try to do what is best." We proceeded. And when it was time for the intercessory prayers, I said something like this:

"One of our members is here today with an especially heavy burden for which we are all asked to pray ...."

The words were no sooner out of my mouth than he stood. And in a voice stronger than my own, said: "I am the man!"

Then followed a dramatic, attentive silence. Calmly he told the story and made his request. More silence. Compassionate silence. Then our prayer. And, after worship ended, intimate surrounding concern, and offers to help.

Sermons often are beat out on the anvil of immediate events, as the times and the timeless intersect and hope is called upon to defeat despair, as life tries one more time to get the best of death.

Other times they survive in states of suspension and dead detachment from where the world really is in its journey, from where the people truly are.

The Holy Spirit waits in the wings.

But the preacher cannot default. He cannot stand there mute, helpless to bring the Word to life. If the Word's servant retreats into the obligation to "say something" because it is Sunday, it is a poor substitute for the passion of proclamation that cannot and will not be stilled.

All who preach, or have preached on any regular basis, will admit to having done both — sometimes from calendared necessity, and other times when the sermon is so electric, so urgent that it writes itself.

And the congregation waits, wondering which today it will be, while out there, half-way to the rear are more than one who wants to cry, "I am the man!" or "I am the woman!" What have you to say to me, what can you say to me about my fears, my job, my alienation from a son that has brought such pain? To sorrow over a husband dead four years that is like an iron weight inside me. To my guilt. To my amazement over the good that keeps pouring through my days and years.

When we who preach come across with the real goods — with something we need to say and want to say — it will be because we have found a way to personalize the truth so that it includes our own blood.

Because we have invaded the present rather than only reviewing the past.

Because we have located whatever it is that connects the hearers to a larger loaf; because our questions, our wonder, our complicity, and our love are also part of the process.

Because we have shared more than ideas. Because we will also have shared the present grace of the living God.

I remember times when none of this happened — at least that's the way it seems now. Over weeks of preparation for a new fall I once became excited by discovering Paul's exhortation to "be holy in every department of your lives." Now here was something to run with, to race with, to tantalize the congregational imagination with, to lead the people along new, secret passageways of the spirit, connectors with eternal things.

The first of the series had been lovingly written and readied for Sunday morning delivery. I picked up the Saturday paper to read how a young civil rights worker had been murdered in Mississippi. Although the next day there were reports of the tragic effect on his family and an increasingly traumatized nation, the sermon stayed mostly as it was. I have never overcome feelings of failure about what I said that morning.

In another parish with a considerable retirement-age constituency, I preached an autumn sermon titled "The November Years." For some it came out sounding as if it were time to see an attorney about drafting a Last Will and Testament. The people's minds were in another place — not contemplating the approach of death, but dwelling on the daily damage wrought by stereotypes of ageism.

Another Sunday I tried to proclaim the salvation gospel through the eyes and experience of three other Christians who had given shape to my own trust in God — G. A. Studdert-Kennedy, Thomas Merton, and Henri J. M. Nouwen. While the effort was noble, I remember talking later with two listeners who had personal agendas of suffering that were light years removed from what I had been talking about.

Yet other Sabbath mornings I seemed to have gotten it right. Sermons titled "Learning To Manage Our Fears" and "What Shall We Do About The Problems We Cannot Do Anything About?" apparently had impact. Another came on that Easter morning when our daughter Susan was killed in an accident on the way home to spend Resurrection Day with us. The sermon (the book came later), with the stolen title, "On A Clear Day You Can See Forever," also seemed to leave the people feeling that I had been speaking directly to them — that God was present in undeniable ways.

Little is here about lectionary preaching. I am not hesitant to affirm its values, so long as it does not become wooden or mechanical. It doesn't have to be. Yet neither does obedience to a lectionary assure anything except a comprehensiveness of approach to what the Bible has to say. One can still preach from a list and wind up fumbling with ashes.

There are too many Sundays on which one feels called to be a persuasive expositor of faith. Sometimes we are too tired to listen to the Voice beyond our own. Sometimes we try too hard to parade our scholarship when a crust of bread is what is needed. Or we may fall in love with our own plans that prevent our hearing the wild winds of humanity or the soft breezes of peace.

But when we stand there and look into those wonderful, waiting faces, and trust the knowledge that we have something to say that must be heard, something that is longing to be heard, something that transcends yesterday's ten o'clock news, something that feeds the soul and comes out of the overflow of our own struggle with God — preaching as programmed obligation dies and the continuing incarnation is confirmed.

I still see, standing up within the congregation, that young man who had told me about his car lurching through the door of a bank building saying, "I am the man!" Like Pilate saying, "Ecce Homo" (behold the man) as he presented Jesus to the crowds. "I am the man" shows up regularly. One waits to see if any word has come that bears his name, a word that is uniquely his own reassurance, or summons to act.

This is a time in which it is easy to be disillusioned about preachers and preaching. We have moved into a new age of communications and of skepticism about those who pretend to higher authority. Even the word "preaching" is made to sound shallow and of limited use in helping people to form decisions or live gallantly.

At its best, though, preaching shatters the routineness. It opens the eyes of second worlds. It becomes a letter from Christ "written not with ink but with the Spirit of the living God, not on tablets of stone, but on tablets of human hearts."

As a long-time admirer of the writer/dramatist Norman Corwin, I once in a moment of boldness mailed him a copy of a book I had written. He was then teaching, as a senior statesman of creative and script writing at the University of Southern California. In acknowledging what I had sent, he said the book had arrived on the day before one of his last classes of the semester — and that he had ended the class by reading aloud from it.

Like a treasured personal letter, we can expect a sermon to be unique to the moment, and as important to those who listen as a love letter is to us in our most tender moments.

That happens when we have had something to say. Something that may not last out the night, but has given someone a few glimpses of stars.

Chapter 4

Windows Of Wonder — Choosing Illustrations That Set Ideas Dancing

I feel life is so small unless it has windows into other worlds.

— Bertrand Russell

"Windows On The World" is the name of a classy restaurant atop the World Trade Tower in New York. It has tall panels of windows, and it is one of the best places — especially around sunset — to see what the Apple looks like from 60 or 70 stories up.

"Windows" is also a metaphor in preaching that describes the role illustrations play in making sermons concrete, powerful, and memorable. They let the light in. Through them we are able to see what is happening inside. Who lives there. How the furniture is arranged. Where the kitchen is, the play room, where to sleep when you are tired.

Balboa Island is accessible from Newport Beach, California, by only one two-lane bridge. Entirely surrounded by the pacific waters of the Pacific Ocean, there are only three or four dozen streets on the island, and many beautiful homes.

Nothing unusual about that. But what is slightly unusual is the tradition which has developed there that all living room drapes are to be left pulled open — even in the evening. A popular walker's pastime is to circle the island a little after sunset and see how the residents are going about life inside their homes.

Except for back-rooms and bedrooms, all is in view. Families at dinner. Rooms looking elegant with polished furniture. Kids watching television. Bridge games. Cocktails with friends. Flower arrangements, curving stairways, paintings and sculptures. Book readers. The "we've got it made" on evening display.

Sermon illustrations will reveal a more ordinary, truthful, and often broken kind of world than this if they are to illuminate what life is all about and are to contribute to the believability of what is being said.

Still, here are a few suggestions about homiletical windows. None is original, but I have come to believe in their value as guidelines, and make use of them over and over again. I won't identify their sources because in most instances I've long since forgotten them — or never knew in the first place. But here they are anyway, and they're free.

Try to have every sermon include what Dr. Ross Snyder called "one big scene." Remain with an illustration once you begin. And whether it is a major or minor one, sufficiently long enough to allow worshippers to see and feel the action involved, its latent emotional power — rather than settling for a two-sentence "passing reference."

Honor the Bible's own treasury of illustrations. But don't be confined to them. Today's world is a different one from the Bible's typically pastoral backdrop. Yet there are biblical ingredients present and constant — in theater, novels, literature, television, news items, hospital wards, travel, the world of science, the life of megacities, and the questions of children.

Honor also the difference between moralizing and giving hearers "struggle room." Preaching isn't serving packaged answers.

Allow your own soul, perplexity or ecstasy to show. But beware of over-reliance on the autobiographical. "Now when I was a boy in Missouri," complained a listener, "got to be awfully old."

Help overcome a "prose-flattened" world by the use of the poetic. Giving credit is important, but sometimes lines need to burst upon the scene, and do their work before anything is said about authorship.

Use aesthetic and visceral references to light up what you are saying, taking care to avoid ornateness or triteness. If we offend, as at times we will, let it be for reasons that reveal faithfulness to the truth.

Let silence become an illustration, too. Let there be times of absorbency. Give silence the opportunity to be "full," not awkward pauses.

Don't embarrass with illustrations that, even by stretching, could reveal a confidence, or to make the congregation worry that they may be in the process of having some of their personal worlds exposed without permission.

Take seriously the first few minutes of the sermon time. It may or may not involve the use of your "one big scene," but always should include some of the best of what the sermon contains.

Illustrate: to make bright. *Luster* (buried within "illustrate"): soft reflected light, sheen, gloss, glorious or radiant quality, splendor (American Heritage Dictionary). Both definitions help explain some of the magic of preaching when a transcendent light is allowed to shine in, through, upon, and past the stuff of daily living.

Windows are in all shapes and tints. They protect. Reveal. Enshrine yesterday and offer vistas of tomorrow. Dance with color. They are friends of the sun, and the trees outside. On dismal, rainy days they are good to stand before, maybe touch with your nose.

Congregations are windows through which we get the chance to recognize practical love at work. They are faith communities that include angels of all ages, of laughter and joined tears, of breaking bread with joy and grief shared beside an open grave. Of Christ risen, of hungry persons fed, the homeless accommodated, of patio sunrises, an open Bible, a tap on or an arm around our shoulder. Churches of resurrection, a community of witnesses, a place of healing, previews of heaven, baptismal waters and wedding vows, struggle and serenity, the prophet's mantle, the banquets of the heart.

Suffering is a well-known window on patience and brilliant courage. Hope is a window on the future. All sermons are windows of meaning, filtered through the passion and the sincerity of the preacher.

> *Lord, how can man preach thy eternal Word?*
>   *He is a brittle, crazy glass;*
> *Yet in thy temple thou dost him afford*
>   *This glorious and transcendent place,*
>   *To be a window through thy grace.*
>
> *But when thou dost anneal in glass thy story,*
>   *Making thy life to shine within*
> *The holy preachers, then the light and glory*
>   *More rev'rent grows, and more doth win;*
>   *Which else shows watrish, bleak, and thin.*
>
> *Doctrine and life, colors and light, in one*
>   *When they combine and mingle, bring*
> *A strong regard and awe; but speech alone*
>   *Doth vanish like a flaring thing*
>   *And in the ear, not conscience, ring.*
>
> — George Herbert (1593-1633)
> "The Windows"

Windows have been opened for me by two modern artists of the imagination.

There's this wonderful story Donald Baillie tells in *Out of Nazareth* that sets up sound waves in the heart.

He was on a late Sunday afternoon walk through the Scottish countryside when he came upon a signpost which pointed the way to a small village he had once heard of, and which had been memorialized in a poem as a tiny out of the way place where nothing ever happened. He wasn't in a hurry so he turned in that direction for a look.

Upon arriving, the first thing that caught his attention was a neat, white church with a small adjoining cemetery, and he wound his way around to the front door to see if there was any notice there about evening worship.

Yes, there would be a service — one around seven. It sounded like that might get him home pretty late, so he decided to move on when he suddenly caught sight of a woman in the cemetery with a bouquet of flowers in her hands. And he wandered over to speak to her.

The two engaged in friendly conversation. Then she told him that the flowers were for the grave of her son who was buried there — who, after he had completed high school, had sat for an examination in a larger adjoining town, and had qualified for a scholarship to Oxford.

The whole village had experienced a burst of pride over that achievement. (People of the town I grew up in felt that way when John Smoller, one of our own, received an appointment to West Point. For our 7,000 inhabitants, it was a distinction comparable to being chosen as an astronaut or winning a Van Cliburn piano competition.)

The young man had excelled at Oxford. But, in the summer before his final year, he had drowned in a boating accident.

This Sunday was the first anniversary of his death. And the service that night was to be a memorial to his brief but splendid young life.

The reason Baillie wrote about this incidental meeting was to call attention to the fact that there are no unimportant places, anywhere. That in all kinds of surprising locations, deep and great human events occur even though the world at large may not notice.

The second story has a California twist:

A certain couple had two children. And the younger daughter took all the money she could find and went to the beach and spent it surfing — sitting on bar stools and living her own life.

She got into Trouble with a capital T.

And when she had spent everything she had — and was hungry and homeless, she became a cook's helper in a wayside diner where she lived on the little she could make, and no one helped her very much.

But one day she woke up. She came to herself and said: "The girl who used to work for us at home had more than I've got. I think I'll call home and tell them I think I've made a big mistake — that I have sinned against them, and against heaven, and against everything I ever heard in Sunday school and church, and that I'm not worth being considered their daughter. I'll ask them to let me come home, though, and I'll work around the house. I'll get a job. I'll do anything. I wonder if they're home now . . . ."

So she went to the booth and reversed the charges, and her mother picked up the phone on the first ring, and her father on the second, because they had been waiting, waiting.

And the daughter said over the phone: "I've been a fool, and I've been bad, and I don't blame you if you don't want to have anything to do with me. I know I'm not worthy to be called your daughter."

But the parents both began to talk at once. And they said, "Oh, we're so glad to hear from you. Tell us where we can pick you up. We'll be there as soon as we can."

So they brought her home, and they got her some decent clothes, and even gave her some heirloom jewelry. They had a family party with the stereo turned way up, and everyone laughed, and it was like old times.

"It was even better than old times," the father said, with his arm around his daughter, "because we thought you might be dead, or worse than dead."

And they began to be merry. Very merry indeed.

Now her older brother had been at work, and he drove into the driveway and said to the first person he saw:

"What's going on?"

And whoever answered him said: "Your sister has come home and they're having barbecued veal out back because she's safe and sound."

But the brother was angry, and he stomped around in the driveway, kicked the tires on his convertible, let out a few curse words, and refused to go in.

After a while, his father came out and said: "Come in, son; sister's home."

But the boy scowled at his dad. "Look," he said, "I've been a good son. I've worked hard, and I've been obedient to you and Mom, and you never even had me and my friends in for hamburgers. But when this daughter of yours — who took half your money, and lived with all those beach bums — when she comes crawling back, you throw a party. What kind of justice is that?"

The father, knowing there was a good bit of truth in what his son said, answered, "Son, you are upset; you forget. We have always been together. You, and your mother and I have lived together in comfort. We've eaten well. Your friends have been our friends. Our home has been theirs. You *have* been a good son. Everything I have is yours, and you know it."

"Forget about *my* daughter. She's *your* sister, and she's come home. She's alive and well in spite of what she has done. She's repentant. She's beaten down. She needs us now, and she needs you. She was as good as dead and is alive. She was lost, and now has been found. Come in, please ..."

Jesus, said Fred Cropp, left the story there.

A legend tells of a boy who looked for some windows of gold which he saw far away "when he looked in the valley at sunrise each day." He set out in search of them, only to discover them at sunset as he started home again, when their light was reflected in the windows of the little cabin from which he had begun the search earlier the same morning.

There are windows through which we catch glimpses of things divine. Some surround the familiar spaces we occupy each day.

Chapter 5

Make Way For Poets Of The Heart

One of the dividends of the ministry is coming to know and enjoy different people — all ages and all human conditions. Often there are surprises.

One came for me on a fall afternoon in the 1960s when some members of my Lexington congregation and I visited a Trappist monastery to see what life is like as a monk. Coming out of the Reformed tradition which has no such orders, I never thought of life behind the walls as anything involving me personally. The silences. Rising at 2 a.m. to pray (after having gone to bed with the sun). A seeming disengagement from social suffering. Celibacy. For most of us, especially for non-Catholics, a strange world.

Which is why we went. To see how those disciples could attract and apply to anyone healthy and fascinated by life's stunning variety. But on the tour bus that day (the 40 of us had been invited to look around and stay for dinner) one began to feel a mysterious, secret attraction.

The inward journey. The career of the soul. Discoveries about God that lie deeper than attending services. Anything that could call up lifelong, life-separating commitment. It was the mystery that prompted Thomas Merton to write *The Seven-Story Mountain,* a book that had so charmed me a dozen years before.

The bus circled in front of the retreat house. We disembarked in the rain and were met by a greeter who also would show us where we could buy cheeses made by the brothers. Wide-smiling, and for the moment out from under his vow of silence, he outlined what we would be doing during the next three or four hours. He then turned us over to Father Louis who would be our guide. He would show us the library, the simple padded sleeping cells, a tool house where farm implements were kept, then to the chapel quickly being absorbed in shadows for one of the last prayer services of the day. Then the common meal with its fascinating hand signals that meant "please pass the bread."

It was an unforgettable experience, and I still find myself thinking about a place called "Gethsemani," a dozen miles or so down a country road east of Bardstown, Kentucky.

Then a stunning discovery: Father Louis *was* Thomas Merton — "Louis" being the religious name he took when he joined the Order. When we got ready to leave about 7:30, I spoke for a few moments with Father Louis, asking if I might some day return and have time to talk to him. Thus began a cherished friendship. The subsequent visit, about a month later, resulted in this original verse:

Meeting With Thomas Merton

Two long rows of September trees, like mower teeth
Clipped the lawn of sky. We sat
Beneath them, on folding chairs (ugly invention),
To pass through our eye-fingers the miracle
Of knowing each other.

I would have studied the roughness and the
Purpose of his leather belt. But his face was
Too interesting for that diversion. Thus, I chose
Excursion into his monkish heart. That's
Why I came to Gethsemani.

"Man's God's trophy," he said. The rest I've mostly
Forgotten. That's quite enough for fourteen lifetimes
To think about. God's trophy. Polished, proud.
But I remembered that sometimes trophies get dropped
And golden heads get broken off.

The private quest — the search through solitariness for immediate communion with God is as old as the Bible itself. It is a road paved with autobiographies of wonder, experimentation, and advice to those who seek that quality in their lives that Paul Tillich called "depth." He once described it as the "missing dimension" in our complex efforts to theologize our way to and through the gates of heaven.

The literature of the Puritans is a large vault of social history. And, while it seems to have lost most of its meaning for these times, "piety" is making a comeback as ceremonial religion is more and more replaced by individuals searching for an Eternal Now that begins to transform life at its center.

It's a little startling to eavesdrop on today's "intentional" communities and hear Protestants speak about spiritual directors, spiritual formation, fasting, journal keeping. Iona and Taizé have been around a long time now. But something new is happening, and the United Church of Christ and the Presbyterian Church (U.S.A.) have established national offices to develop programs to provide support for this growing interest in a spirituality that seeks some middle ground between a separateness — the solitary pathway of the heart — and the Life Together, which Dietrich Bonhoeffer eloquently described, and which Paul appears to make basic to his portrait of Christian behavior in 1 Corinthians 12.

The Church (note the word is singular) does not regard this as an alien movement. But, so far as I can tell, this rediscovery is being carried on with little reference to the preaching event, or where kerygma fits into our hunger for Brother Lawrence's kitchen.

Is it because the path is so private — where finding a way to make oneself accountable for the stewardship of such a mystic potential becomes achievable only when applied to one other person? Where most pain and the gain involves lonely struggle or individual ecstasy? Where meditation risks getting separated from the prayers of the people, and the sacramental character of the commonplace is forfeited in the pursuit of the discipline for discipline's sake?

That sounds hostile. And shouldn't be — after my own spirit-shaping experiences of reading (in addition to *Seven-Story Mountain*), Thomas Kelly's *Testament Of Devotion, John Woolman's Journal,* Luther's *A Simple Way To Pray, The Ladder Of Devotion* by Caspar Calvor, the writings of John Watson, the Scriptures themselves. My inner life has been made indescribably rich by encounters with God in places other than a room full of pews.

Yet there is a connectionalism here that makes me want to come to the defense of the sermon, keeping preaching tightly bound up with the assignment to hear and do the will of God.

Biblical models for true spirituality come alive through preaching.

Preaching furnishes the vision of community without which the inward quest is distorted. And there is a need for contemporaneity which informed preaching supplies and which is missing if we try to make the journey alone.

Preaching is validation when God is experienced both through knowledge and through action.

Culture needs the influence both of itineraries by those who have experienced God through prayer and by those who have known God and God's support in the struggle for greater justice on Earth.

The Royalty Of The Pulpit was the title of a book written earlier in the century about who had been leading preachers of the times. I never owned the book. Neither have I forgotten that title.

Royalty suggests superior status of some sort — pomp and circumstance, recognition, sovereignty. Pulpit "royalty" suggests that "these were among the best." Such a roll call of heroes will be forever changing and, to some degree, indexed to culture (if popularity is the yardstick). Yet it will also transcend the fickleness of the moment in ways that have us remembering their gifts to persons like me in whom their wisdom, vision, and greatness lives on.

There are the classical preachers whose reputations were established between pre-Reformation times and the Reformation.

An impressive nineteenth century list of those who made Scotland synonymous with the power of preaching to help set the nation's character or, in the New World, determine the outcome of its civil war. Then, somewhere in the first third of the present century, other changes came along such as the science versus religion debate and the widened acceptance of textual criticism. The resurgence of topical (vs. textual) preaching, with the free church, yoked ecstasy to activism, the Niebuhrian approach to ethics, and new understandings of what faithful living is all about.

Among some of my own best models, beginning with the year I was born, 1920, have been G. A. Studdert-Kennedy, Harry Emerson Fosdick, Leslie Weatherhead, E. Stanley Jones, Ralph Sockman, George Buttrick, Peter Marshall, Donald Baillie, James Stewart, and Arthur John Gossip.

To allow myself the luxury of a second decalogue, I also name Louis Evans, Carlyle Marney, James Pike, Ted Loder, Wallace Hamilton, Gerald Kennedy, Eugene Carson Blake, Liston Pope, Elton Trueblood, and Richard Raines.

Plus the following, whose writing informed my mind and added muscle and music to my faith: Loren Eiseley, Thomas Merton, Halford Luccock, Reinhold Niebuhr, Frederick Buechner, Walter Brueggemann, C. S. Lewis, Robert McAfee Brown, Ernest Fremont Tittle, John Sutherland Bonnell, Henri J. M. Nouwen, Howard Thurman, Samuel Miller, David H. C. Read, Joseph Ford Newton, Ernest Campbell, William Sloane Coffin, John Henry Jouette, Ernest Gordon, and Abraham Heschel.

I wish these lists included the Afro-American preachers (whom we know are among the best preachers in the world), women clergy (they are already proving that the future will be theirs!), Hispanic minds and voices (leading the revival of preaching in the Southern hemisphere), Native American and Asian servants of the word (like Kagawa).

I can't change that. I can only hope for some balance by the willingness to share what has flowed into my inner world from so many sources — their passion, hallowed imaginations, knowledge of the world, their books, their poetry, their ability to move life forward, to teach and to care, to finish in their own way the prayer "Lord, make me an instrument of your peace."

Preachers, of course, do not preach to be honored or even remembered. And even to suggest such a "Royalty of the Pulpit" sounds silly, and at odds with the humility of the One whose life, death, and resurrection we are called to proclaim.

Yet the heart keeps a scrapbook.

And there is gratitude to those who have opened our eyes, been our teachers and guides and, having received the torch of hope from someone else who handed it on, evoked in us an inevitable remembrance, and resistance to forgetting.

The day of the "big steeple" preachers seems to be over. As over as solemn sabbaths and worship centers in our homes. Occasionally a sermon makes the news, but that occurs when ecclesiastical authority is threatened, the sermon is connected with scandal, or immorality is condemned as unacceptable in this society.

And preaching, from what I have been able to tell in my limited visits, is nearly over in Europe.

In an American city on Sunday morning, suburbia may present another kind of evidence.

Where we are most apt to find preaching "thriving" is in the new mega-congregations on the edge of the larger metropolitan areas where belief structures are mostly left undefined, but sprawling parking lots, abundant child care, and family support services have made these congregations the "right" place to be — congregations where preachers have little in common with what this chapter is about.

Trouble within monarchies has given royalty a bad name of late, but "royal" still sets up within us bright colors, majestic songs, beauty, life understood as pageantry. This too is what preaching is about, as through the life of Jesus, Thomas Merton, and some of the rest of us, new worlds await their realization. Faith in a Spirit that combines power with love, and love with power, makes the future look more promising than we may have thought.

46

Chapter 6

To See Your Face Is Like Seeing The Face Of God

If you could deliver one sermon, what would you speak about? Though the question sounds trite, it has sometimes been asked of most preachers — usually in a half-serious way. What text, truth, or character has come to fill your heart's imagination, changed your life, or made you eager to use one big chance to share it with others?

For me, the answer is in the story of the reconciliation in the desert between Esau and Jacob, years after the stealing of the birthright, where, comforted by Esau's forgiveness, Jacob says: "To see your face is like seeing the face of God."

I have fallen in love with this part of the Genesis narrative because it is filled with echoes and the images of having so often seen, during the years of my active ministry, the face of God in the faces of others. We say of Jesus that faith enables us to see in his face the human face of God, which may come as close to expressing his divine nature as we can get.

By my early 20s much had happened that brought me face to face with God on more than one occasion.

• I walked beside George Washington Carver, the African-American agricultural genius, in a Simpson College baccalaureate parade and heard him describe his intimate dialogue with "Mr. Creator." Carver was a deeply spiritual, self-made man who, in spite of racist opposition, became one of the world's most distinguished botanists.

• I entered law school and began to see God at work in ways and places and people and history that dissolved all false boundaries between the secular and the sacramental.

47

• I was married in 1942, as a commissioned ensign, soon after Pearl Harbor. I had taken vows at the old Chicago Post Office to help defend the country against all enemies, foreign and domestic. Yet love's vows have always seemed like the most important, and the years that followed, including the births of our four children, produced their own solemn, beautiful moments of grace.

• I had my first up-close assignment with death — death on the high seas. Our American destroyer, *The USS Moffett*, was assigned to anti-submarine patrol in the South Atlantic Ocean. It was May 1943. A German submarine had attacked a convoy of Allied ships, and a call had gone out for help. *Moffett* was soon on its way and the crew placed on General Quarters, the ship's highest state of battle readiness. As we reached the location on the navigational chart where the marauders supposedly had been sighted, the South Atlantic waters were blue and unruffled, and the sun was shining brightly overhead. But within less than an hour all that changed. Depth charges launched in strategic patterns sent geysers high into the air, and spread lethal shrapnel fires beneath.

More minutes passed.

More depth charges dropped and spouted.

Then, out of Neptune's chambers there arose, dragon-like, the gray prey, as the enemy submarine's crew manned the deck guns and brought our ship under brief but withering fire. Then the ocean became blood. The submarine was abandoned, leaving two dozen crew adrift in yellow life vests, each stenciled with swastikas. Later there would be a sunset burial of all the dead. And along with other of our own young officers I would move among the survivors held in the mess halls, looking into their equally young faces — Esau and Jacob — hoping our failure to live in understanding and peace might be converted into some better peace for tomorrow.

Written years later on a passage to England aboard the *S.S. France,* these words of mine kept me remembering some of the unusual places where the face of God shines unexpectedly upon us:

Chapel On Board Ship

Why does it seem strange to find
You here, O Lord? You who
Knew the sea, and loved it well.
The swell of the waves you understood.
Their power you once did bind.

This shiny, stained-glass stall
Was built for you, they say.
The cross is here, and a place
To kneel. Here today, I sought
Your face; and, yes, I heard You call.

But out there, thick with salt and flimsy foam
I think I see a crowded boat
With twelve rough men and ageless Love.
The Chapel door I close (with thanks).
And try to hitch-hike home.

• When we were living in Lexington, our three-year-old
son whom we called Jamie, later Jim, developed a case of croup
one evening after most of the family was in bed. We did all
we could to relieve the wheezing and gasping for breath. We
walked him, turned on the shower, hoping steam would help.
But his condition seemed only to worsen. At midnight we were
beginning to feel desperate and telephoned Dr. William Maxson for advice.

Were there any pharmacies open at that time of night, and
could he call in a prescription?

Yes, there was one. And yes, he could.

I got into our car and went roaring down the deserted
streets. Within a half hour I was back with the coveted reme-
dy. Relieved, but also surprised to see Dr. Maxson standing
in the front hallway, attired in bathrobe, bedroom slippers,
and a scarf thrown around his neck. The answer to the fears
of two very frightened young parents.

Bill Maxson was bald, at times almost severe looking, but
inwardly golden and good. Seeing him there in the doorway
at 1 a.m. gave me one more unforgettable glimpse of the face
of God.

• There was an earlier glimpse, too. It was my 19th birthday and I was a college junior. I had been allowed the use of my dad's car for the fall semester, so four of us celebrated with a picnic at Water Works Park, a few miles south of Indianola, Iowa. We were Virginia, my main and lifetime love interest, and I; and another couple, Wayne and Letha. As Maurice Chevalier would put it, "I remember it well."

We were in a celebrative mood and had a lot of fun along the banks of the stream that divides the park. Around nine o'clock we repacked our picnic basket and started back to town along the same dark, narrow road that had brought us. I was driving.

So was a man, named Fred Hutchcroft, but in an opposite direction. His farm bordered the road. Because he had seen a light in one of his fields, he had set out to investigate, driving slowly along the dirt edge, on the lookout for intruders.

We approached each other near the crest of a hill steep enough to observe the headlight beams of both cars, but too late to avoid a collision that shattered not only the quiet of a cool October evening, but also the steel and glass hood, radiator, and windshields of both vehicles.

I got out of my father's car and asked this stranger if he was hurt.

"I don't know," he said, "how about you?"

Inside our 1938 Chevrolet with its once brightly polished but now-mangled front, there were no sounds, no pleas for help nor moans of pain. Only three crumpled human forms on upholstery smeared with blood. I alone remained conscious — stunned and frightened. Mr. Hutchcroft had disappeared, the road soaked up in the night.

I took my three unconscious companions and laid them beyond further danger, after trying to see if anyone could speak or had any idea about what had happened. But they were all as silent as the stars. If I prayed, I don't remember it. I only recollect starting to walk back along the way we had come — fighting back 19-year-old tears. Then breaking into a run.

Another car approached, slowing when its occupants saw me, and inside there was a warm, wonderful woman's face, with lovely auburn hair. I remember it wreathed the moment as she asked, "Are you in trouble? What can we do to help?" I saw the face of God that night. The face of a human angel. Some of the injuries were serious, but we all survived. A trial later vindicated my car handling in spite of my age.

God as a Rescuer is not that rare for anyone who has come from the darkness into light again.

James Stephens describes another form of identification, this one closer to that famous wrestling match between Jacob and an adversary who, it turns out, was also on a heavenly assignment.

> *I saw God! Do you doubt it?*
> *Do you dare to doubt it?*
> *I saw the Almighty Man! His hand*
> *Was resting on a mountain! And*
> *He looked upon the World, and all about it:*
> *I saw Him plainer than you see me now*
> *— You mustn't doubt it!*
>
> *He was not satisfied!*
> *His look was all dissatisfied!*
> *His beard swung on a wind, far out of sight*
> *Behind the world's curve! And there was light*
> *Most fearful from His forehead! And He sighed —*
> *That star went always wrong, and from the start —*
> *I was dissatisfied! —*
>
> *He lifted up His hand!*
> *I say He heaved a dreadful hand*
> *Over the spinning earth! Then I said, — Stay,*
> *You must not strike it, God! I'm in the way!*
> *And I will never move from where I stand! —*
> *He said, — Dear child, I feared that you were dead, —*
> *... And stayed His hand!*

> — James Stephens
> "What Tomas Said in a Pub"

51

I began by talking about a favorite text that keeps drawing me back, a Scripture that keeps playing familiar music inside my soul.

As I look forward to the completion of my own life, so beautifully satisfying, so rich in human relationships, a cup that has overflowed, then overflowed some more, a gift beyond anyone's deserving — let this part of the story end by remembering these two other personally favorite verses:

> *You will do well to pay attention to this as to a lamp shining in a dark place, until the day dawns and the morning star rises in your hearts.* — 2 Peter 1:19 (RSV)

And from the second letter to the Corinthians:

> *It is the God who said, "Let light shine out of darkness" who has shone in our hearts to give the light of the knowledge of the glory of God in the face of Jesus Christ.* — 2 Corinthians 4:6 (NRSV)

Chapter 7

Assists From Broadway

Authors regularly use what they refer to as a "hook" to engage the attention of readers quickly. Speakers do the same with listeners.

Sometimes current events serve that purpose. A dramatic moment of the Biblical story will often hustle everyone on board. A new book, film, or popular song may set the stage for deeper listening, if true listening has already begun.

The following sermon was preached at the ordination of Karen Cobb Cadman. It draws upon songs from the Broadway musical *A Chorus Line* to engage the listeners and to deepen their understanding.

Another Chorus Line

Ordination, it has been suggested, is not just a service for the laying on of hands but also for the raising of hands. "Here am I," it says. "Send me."

And it involves us in that most fundamental of all mysteries: revelation.

How is it that people like ourselves come in contact with the living God? How do time and eternity get cross-pollinated with each other? And how are we called out of ho-humness, deadness of soul, and shaped into ships driven by the winds of the Spirit?

In a beautiful little book by Robert Hudnut titled *This People, This Parish,* the writer shows us the universality of the need.

I come and go across the face of this parish. One morning a baby is born. Two mornings later a woman dies. A couple comes to get married. A man goes to the hospital for tests. A woman describes the death of her child. A young woman graduates at the head of her class. A man is on his way to becoming president of a great corporation. Another loses his job.

It is the ebb and flow of our life together. This people, this parish is like a great sea heaving, the tides strong and the currents swift. In every home, as I go down the street tonight, some frail craft is plying that sea between sorrow and joy. The doors open, and I am asked in.

Can it be that people invite the pastor in because they want to share their laughter and their tears? I think so. But there is more to it than that. They invite the pastor because at times they long for the transcendent. They yearn for something more in their lives.

The reason doors open to pastors is that people want to live full lives. They are not content with plying the Atlantic. They want the Pacific, too.

Today I want to ask you to think of the Church into which you are about to be ordained as part of the divine Answer and to share with you something I read in *The New York Times.* On April 28, 1990, at the Schubert Theater, after 15 years and 6,137 performances, the fantastically successful show, *A Chorus Line,* ended in the midst of nostalgia, tears, cheers, applause, and that special magic reserved for opening and closing nights.

Its songs have sung their way permanently into our hearts where they will brighten our living for generations yet to come. Titles and lines like "What I Did For Love," "Kiss the day goodbye and point me toward tomorrow," and "One" all seem like sub-themes of the Christian life. If a song like "One . . .

singular sensation'' seems inappropriate for a day when we should be thinking about theology, biblical exegesis, and polity, consider this: "We are a chorus line, too, equipped with basin and towel, rather than top hat and cane.''

We don't march or kick our legs like Rockettes in symmetrical rhythm. We're a little too stiff and diversified for that. But we form another unbroken line of one as followers of the true Dancer — reaching back to the disciples. Back to that incredible idea that God is actively busy in history. That creation is far from over. That we are not cardboard figures lining pews, but a community of sequined, high steppers, not unlike dancers who strutted their way across the stage that April night in 1990. We are not the original cast. We are, however, the spiritual descendants of that first cast who crossed the stage.

Like those 17 aspiring young actors trying to win one of the eight coveted places in the final cut, our stories are bound together by One Script: the Kingdom of God has come among you.

Or think about some of the show's other lyrics that relate to a life of daring faith. "What I Did For Love" evokes lines like these: "See what love the Father has given us, and so we are loved,'' and "This is love, not that we loved God, but that God has loved us.'' This love that will not let us go, will not let us down, and will not let us off. Perhaps it is more God's song than it is ours.

It is what the Bible is basically about, and what we are about.

"What I Did For Love" is the centerpiece of Christian apologetics, the heart of all meaning.

Muse still one more time upon this magnificent song line: "Kiss the day goodbye and point me toward tomorrow.''

"Forgetting what lies behind and reaching forward to what lies ahead, let us press on toward the prize.''

"Abraham, go out to a land that I will show you.''

And please God, point *us* to tomorrow. That's a prayer to begin each day with, including this special ordination day

55

that sets aside this young woman's life for lifelong service as a faithful minister of Jesus Christ.

But it is that final number "One" that electrifies our feelings and makes us want to jump out of bed — that "one singular sensation" — life flowing toward a crowning moment of ecstasy, whether we call it cross or resurrection, earth or heaven. Each of us is a single unrepeatable, non-interchangeable invention of the one God. If you can believe that with all your heart and soul, life will never defeat you.

"There is One Lord, One Faith, One God and Father of us all — who is in all and through all."

And "We who are many are One in Christ."

At a recent Notre Dame commencement, Sister Thea, who died of cancer at the age of 52, a black woman and a member of one of the Catholic orders, just before her death quoted Sojourner truth, saying, "I'm not going to die. I'm going home like a shooting star." Part of her witness against bigotry at the commencement honor ceremony included her personal credo: "Be black, be white, be man, be woman, be single, be married. But *be* with your whole life, and *be* one with Christ."

Karen, you are called to be one of God's choreographers, to help us all move through life with greater courage, grace, and hope. We feel in our bodies the music for which we were created. We believe that we are meant to understand life as theater — ourselves, not as customers waiting in line to buy tickets, but actors waiting in the wings to be called.

Your task is the same as Gary Collins', whose dossier caught the attention of a particular pastoral Nominating Committee because it included these words about himself: "Without a lively faith on my own part, my role in the congregation's life is likely to be defined as the oiling of an institutional machine." He also wrote, "My role as a pastor is to advance the gospel before God's people in a way that demands a relationship with the living Christ, that summons us to have a common vision and to be faithful in all things."

The ministry of word and sacrament is not the authority of superior wisdom. It's not a white collar, an oversized ring, or a certificate on the wall. It is not the authority to put Reverend before your name or the right to officiate marriages. It is the authority of the pastor servant.

According to Tom Long of Princeton, it belongs to someone who, on behalf of the entire congregation, struggles with the scriptures and with the question, "Is there some word of God we can hear that can change our lives and launch us out among new galaxies of awareness and experience still unnamed?"

Frederick Buechner says, "The job of preachers is to tell the truth, to tell it first in silence, acknowledging that we are not those people who have all the answers, that there is a visible absence of God that we are foolish to deny."

"If the preacher doesn't see or own up to that," he said, "who will take it seriously in trying to proclaim the invisible presence of a risen Christ whose cues we may miss because he is forever surprising us with what he can do with our lives, like the miracles our lives represent to one another?"

Karen, I hope you will always possess deep affection for this ministry to which you are called. And also for the church that will proclaim through you a gospel of responsibility and accountability, a broad and honest justice, sacrifice, and reconciliation of human differences. But we are also directors of the dance, posting notices of rehearsal and asking people to kick their legs higher than they thought they could. We help people keep in love with life and with the God who gives them life.

Your role is to announce that there is both an inward and outward journey and that we are made for both: those who try not only with their lips, but also with their lives.

May the outside poster announce: We are ambassadors of Christ. Those who believe continue to make God's own appeal through us.

Dance then wherever you may be;
I am the Lord of the Dance said he.
And I'll lead you all wherever you may be,
And I'll lead you all in the Dance said he.

A Postscript

Following are some quickly recognizable song titles, which seemed to have a remarkable appropriateness about them on more than one Sunday morning, and helped to establish the theme, which moved from lyrical beauty to theological truth and forms of the Word people were hungry to hear:

"Guess Who's Coming To Dinner?"	(Communion)
"Love Among The Ruins"	(Good Friday)
"Encounters Of The Third (Best) Kind"	(Incarnation)
"Lost In The Stars"	(Psalm 8)
"Ordinary People"	(Sainthood)
"On The Road Again"	(Emmaus)
"The Wind Beneath My Wings"	(Spirit of God)
"Like A Bridge Over Troubled Waters"	(Salvation)
"Inn Of The Sixth Happiness"	(Pilgrimage)

Chapter 8

The Aim Of Preaching: To Bestow The Kiss Of Life

The Los Angeles summer of 1965 produced the frustration-generated Watts riots — or Watts "revolt" as I was taught to call those days. That was the year our family went to England for a pulpit exchange. We were in London the day after Adlai Stevenson dropped dead on Oxford Street, the victim of a heart attack. Mr. Stevenson never became president, but he won a special place in the hearts of the American people. Those of us old enough to remember his campaigns will never forget him — especially the night he lost to Dwight Eisenhower and went on television with his concession statement, quoting from President Lincoln's story about the boy who stubbed his toe and said that he was too big to cry, and far too badly hurt to laugh.

That day is an easy one for me to remember because of the way the afternoon papers reported the incident. The headline used a phrase I had never heard before, though I think the British understood it clearly. I still see those big, black letters on the front page: "Adlai Stevenson Dies — The Kiss of Life Fails."

We would have said CPR.

Now it's Easter Sunday night. In a house with the doors locked. Jesus bestows upon those to whom the work of the kingdom would be committed the "kiss of life," telling us that he "breathed upon" the disciples and said "receive the Holy Spirit." Of the four gospel writers, only John includes this splendid detail.

59

Part of what brings us to worship is the need to have our lives reopened to the Spirit of God, whether we image that as a dove that descends upon our lives, or as a presence we feel in the early evening as we walk along the ocean with the sun falling into the distant horizon, or as huge forces out of control.

God may also seem vividly present to us as we enter upon new forms of experience. Like a first week at college — feeling alone, yet not alone. When two people marry. Or when a child is born, an event that starts the world over. God swoops, slides, or sneaks mysteriously into our common life and life is suddenly different.

The breath of God. The breath of amazement. Of our best selves. Or of refreshment after days or weeks of vacation.

Wrote New Jersey poet Joseph Auslander: "I never pass a steeple by, but I must stop a while and linger, and catch my breath to see the sky take hold of prayer's tremendous finger."

Another word for breath is "inspire" — to breathe into. And when others inspire us, they impart their own kiss of life, usually without realizing what they are doing.

Our country has its own yearnings for new breath. Which may be making the focus too small. Maybe we should think not just about this land, but about a whole society struggling for rebirth, or a planet trying to get its respiratory system going again after finding out how environmentally threatened we seem to be.

Our malaise is deeper than economic.

We know that.

We admit it.

The end of the Cold War wiped out a large territory of meaning that we are still adjusting to. Space adventuring had us turned on for a time, but, breathtaking as it all is, even the exploration of the heavens has lost much of its power to get us up on our feet cheering new victories. Pride, eloquently expressed by the Statue of Liberty, has lapsed into arguments over multiculturalism. Candidates running for office talk much about change. But change of itself is neutral. We are waiting for Godot, but not sure we would recognize him if he appeared.

Yet we remain sure of this: That if our will fails, if our imagination remains impoverished, if we cannot find ways to stop ourselves from killing each other and get our moral nerve back, a basic dream may die.

And where we are trying to get back to is to being a people who are not intimidated by our times, and who would not trade places with any other people or time in history.

So we pray: God breathe upon us once more and save us from becoming a silent valley of bleached bones.

During the same trip that took us to London, then to Wakefield, England, to live for six weeks and to relearn a few things about the War of the Roses and the Royal Duke of York, we had stopped in New York to show our kids some of the special sights there, including a by-night look at the big city from the top of the Empire State Building.

There, at the top, I found a plaque on which these words by MacKinley Kantor had been inscribed — and which I copied down in the poor light:

> *Whence rise you, Lights? From this tower built upon Manhattan's native rock. Its roots are deep below forgotten musket balls, the mouldered wooden shoe, the flint, the bone. What mark you, Lights? Our Nation's doorway. Who sleep or toil beneath your good warm gaze? All who love this land: they who are of the Land's stout seed, and they who love the land because they chose to come. Sing you a song, proud lights? We sing silently. We chant a Mass and Spiritual, Doxology, and Kol Nidre, wheat and cotton, turbine, oil, and golden rod, the wildest mountains and the cities roar. This is a strange new time, Strong Lights, why never do you fear? There is something more powerful: the heart and soul of all Mankind. What build you with your beams? A bridge to the stars. What offer you to God, O Lights? America's devotion.*

There's a saving optimism wrapped up within those words and phrases we may have lost. But it's not too late. Only too late if we give up on our ability to accommodate the kinds of changes that have brought us a new world of women, new worlds of opportunity for disabled persons, and for those who are sexually oriented in ways different from ourselves — perhaps even the faint beginnings of the end of racisms that have poisoned thinking for almost as long as people looked at each other and noticed that they were different — differences that are intentional, beautiful, given of God, good that we change into the opposite of good.

And truth and love abide. Forgiveness abides.

We can make the world young and kind again.

A renewed nation, of course, must consist of renewed people — convinced that they are and can make the difference. This is always part of our agenda as we reassemble in our churches each fall to pray, study, act, and try to determine what part each of us can play as tippers of the balances toward a society reconciled and whole.

It has been said that it is no tragedy to die. Only tragic if we allow wonderful things to die within us while our hearts go on pumping away without our having been animated and refreshed by the kiss of life, which is what preaching is mainly all about.

For a year now I have been putting up a fight against cancer. And so many have supported and encouraged me in that struggle. Such battles wind up making people like myself newly aware of how many people there are who have the same adversary, or many that are worse. But also how aliveness of soul and aliveness to God are not dependent upon receiving favorable treatment at the hands of a life process that defies rational explanation. One of the oldest truths we have is that the best nobilities are frequently exhibited by those who suffer the most. We see their courage and, slightly ashamed, embrace our own tomorrows with thanksgiving.

So we will go on praying and working for a revived nation, attempting to be part of the implementation of our own petitions by being alive to the grandeur of the world itself, alive to the differences that keep it interesting, alive to children, alive to love, and to the divine within the ordinary — the kinds of awareness that prompted Edna St. Vincent Millay to write: "God, I can push the grass apart, and lay my finger on Thy heart."

The church, too, is on its own quest for renewal. Statistics about growth, if Presbyterians are normative, continue to be dismal. But if I had my life to live over, I would want to repeat the course in much the same way, and keep the church as the compass of my existence — a place not where answers are kept in a vault, but where people practice faith, grow in wisdom, and work for justice in ways that keep us restless so long as so few have so much, and so many so little.

In an essay former *Time* editor, Henry Grunwald, looked ahead to the end of this fabulous century, and reflected on what were, or are, the most notable developments of this particular moment of history. While two of his observations didn't surprise me, the third one did.

The first event was the communism which has deeply affected everything else that has gone on in the Western world since 1918.

The second was the new globalism that is already busy replacing national and regional economies — and general thinking — with a new world economy and point of view. Teilhard du Chardin, it appears, was right from an evolutionary standpoint. There *is* evidence that after eons of diversification, Life now seems to be on a course of convergence and reunification. A simple one-celled beginning that became a complex multiverse is trying to become a universe again.

But it was the third that really surprised me. He wrote that we now come to the conclusion that life is a spiritual enterprise for which no secular achievement, no source of pleasure, and no material convenience is a substitute.

A Walter Brueggemann book titled *Finally Comes The Poet* borrows its name from a passage in Walt Whitman's *Leaves of Grass* that offers a hopeful note to end on.

After the seas are all cross'd, (as they seem already
    cross'd,)
After the great captains and engineers have accomplish'd
    their work,
After the noble inventors, after the scientists, the chemist,
    the geologist, ethnologist,
Finally shall come the poet worthy of that name,
The true son of God shall come singing his songs.
                                    — Walt Whitman

"As the Father has sent me, now I send you." And when he had said that, he breathed on them. And gave to them new gifts of power and love. "Receive the Holy Spirit," he said.

That should be enough to make us more than conquerors. And in the fullness of time to fit us for eternal life within an eternal kingdom.

Chapter 9

Welcoming The New Millennium

At a wedding I attended 50 years ago, the bride's brother sang a love song, "At Dawning." I was the groom, and have since forgotten the lyrics. But even the words of the title have a nice sound.

Dawn is a gorgeous time of day. Drenched in pastel beauty, mist, and quiet, it comes very softly, even as the freeways begin their hum of first traffic. For ships at sea, it is a time to do important navigational work. Sailors call it "morning twilight."

And though the twenty-first century is still a few heartbeats away, there's a feeling its dawn has already begun. Already we are standing at the edge of tomorrow looking steadily across a narrowing divide.

When Eugene Carson Blake was a chief spokesperson for Protestant Christianity in the early sixties, he made a trip to Korea where he visited a number of congregations in a gesture of spiritual solidarity. His mission accomplished, he met with a few local leaders the night before his scheduled return to the United States. They suggested a 5:30 a.m. "prayer meeting" as a send-off before catching his plane to fly out towards the morning sun. Blake thought it was a fine idea, though was surprised that the location for the gathering was an outdoor athletic stadium. He expected maybe two dozen to show up. That morning, as the sky began to change color, 9,000 Christians met to sing hymns and to express their gratitude for his coming.

There is, of course, something timeless about the agenda of preaching. But as 2000 A.D. comes ever closer, the end of a millennium appears to call for extraordinary reflection. It demands new thought about what is going on in history. It requires fresh perspective on what this both tragic and exciting century, now ending, means within the Greater Scheme, and on what new priorities the new age, about to be born, deserves.

In Thornton Wilder's Prologue to *The Eighth Day* (1967), there's a splendid fictional description of what went on in Coaltown, Illinois, around midnight on December 31, 1899. People gathered in front of the courthouse clock to cry, and sing — not "Auld Lang Syne," but "Our God, Our Help In Ages Past." And how once the community welcome of 1900 was over, Dr. Gillies, town physician, acknowledged to be the wisest man in town, met with a small group in the local tavern and responded to their questions. There's too much of what he said to be quoted, but a few of Dr. Gillies' "answers" send the mind on journeys.

Acknowledging a need for optimism, he said, "It is the duty of old men to lie to the young. Let them encounter their own disillusions," he said. "We strengthen our souls, when young, on hope; the strength we acquire enables us later to endure despair as a Roman should."

He continued: "The process of life never stands still. The creation has not come to an end. Man is not an end but a beginning. We are at the beginning of the second week — the children of the Eighth Day."

When Anne Lindbergh was trying to regain her soul along the shores of Captiva Island and wrote those superb essays in *Gift From The Sea* about her pilgrimage — using the images of sea shells — she said it was "along toward the middle of the second week" that she started to come alive again.

Perhaps we are the children of the *Ninth* Day, if Dr. Gillies was correct, with more new chapters of the Creation Story about to begin on January 1, 2000.

It's hard, though, to bid adieu to an era that has witnessed a thousand revolutions, spawned a dozen new forms of freedom. Still it is — and always has been — Good-bye Forever.

I wrote a poem by that name, remembering the sentiments of leaving home for college.

'Twill only be for a year, Mother, that I must leave.
And the scholarship — it will help me learn so much.
And I will learn; I will pass all the examinations. Then,
After one year, I will return to you. Wait for me.

Good-bye, my son; good-bye forever. And thank you
for the love that will take the scarlet wounds of life's
New loneliness, and fill them with the oil
Of knowing that this is the price of a man.

The volumes of forecast have already begun to appear, furnished with awesome things to come, miracles stacked one on top of the other, scenarios that both dazzle and warn, and make us glad it will be others and not us who will be stuck with the problems "progress" brings.

Preachers of the new millennium will see older nationalistic loyalties dissolved, the Third World merged with the rest of us. The magic word will not be computers, but genetics. People will continue to regard 100 years as a normal lifetime, yet disease will get in its familiar innings. AIDS will become a terrible thing from out of our past but other battles will replace those dreadful letters, "HIV-Positive." Space won't fascinate the imagination the way it did during the twentieth century, but we will keep learning more and more about how all things began, and what is cosmologically possible as space platforms turn operational — soon to be as routine as the 1980-90 shuttles. We will continue to delight in convenience and speed, but be gradually dissuaded from letting them become ends in themselves.

Five great Imperishables of the Spirit persist. Belief:
- In the Permanence of God.
- That Life is a sacred journey and involves our choice.
- In the undisputed supremacy of love.
- That God is knowable; that faith risks being wrong.
- That Life has a transcendent dimension and is transformed by encounters, both human and divine.

The church will continue because it has an Eternal agenda. Its institutional decay may continue, but an exclusively materialistic existence will self-destruct on Empty, and we will press the search beyond Lexus automobiles, second homes with jaccuzis, and the idolatry of leisure and exemptions from responsibility. We will never be able to shake off the call of holiness.

The pressure of population and environmental integrity will make community less and less optional if there is to be survival for any.

In 1830, after five billion years of existence, the world population was one billion. A hundred years later, in January 1930, we became two billion. In 1960, when John F. Kennedy and Richard Nixon were vying for the presidency, the figure became three billion. In 1975, four billion. Today there are 5.7 billion of us. And by 2000, 6.3 billion. So that more than half of all the people who *ever* lived on planet Earth are alive today.

We might wish there were some sort of intrinsic magic to the flip of a calendar page — that the heavens would let out a gasp, that God would speak, and the world would be suddenly different. We know, without waiting to read it here, that in that moment, the sun will rise and set with the same regularity as it did the day before. It will not be marked by the tolling of any Great Clock. Rather, it will be a day to be born, or die, to begin to plan high school graduation, schedule a wedding, or sign up for try-outs on Broadway.

In the waning days of the twentieth century, we have found ourselves meditating even more than usual upon the Meaning of Time. But whatever that is, it hasn't changed. A trillion seconds equals 33,750 years. Light still travels at 186,000 miles per second.

Only what we *do* with time transforms a blank canvas into wild streaks of color and meaning, and maybe those meanings are the only things that really endure.

Looking back, 1000 A.D. produced these accomplishments: Leif Ericson reached Nova Scotia; an Indian mathematician,

Sridhara, recognized the importance of the zero; there were several abortive attempts to fly; potatoes and corn were planted in Peru, the Chinese invented gunpowder; the Saxons settled in Bristol; and because it was the end of the millennium, there was widespread fear of the end of the world.

2,000 A.D. should produce a more impressive list. The world has speeded up. We are smarter, richer, much better equipped to explore what the world is all about than we were a thousand years ago. But we are also more dangerous to ourselves, more conceited — and less inclined to be kind and tolerant.

Dawn is a good time to be thinking about such things as we bask in the newness of another new beginning and restudy our dreams. Lifting up still one more prayer for peace, and, for the ten-millionth time, go about the business of sorting out the permanent and the beautiful from the impermanent and the ugly.

We wish for a more settled order, but the chaos that has followed what appeared to be the end of the Cold War is enough to prove to us that we will have to wing our way into tomorrow just like those who were around to begin this century for us.

As the '60s came to an end, someone wrote:

> *The face of change is a young one — and it comes in many colors. All previous revolutions had, as their goal, the attainment of some new state of equilibrium. What we are seeing in our time is a new order of revolution, whose goal is not a new equilibrium but social disorder itself. It is the first social recognition that* continuous change itself is a form of equilibrium *(emphasis added), and that it is only in disorder that we find order. You can't have fun surfing on a slow wave, and you can't surf at all on a frozen one.*

Yet in the midst of this uproar we still find a compass in the music of George Frederic Handel and Ludwig von Beethoven; and the heart of Nature in the sound of the sea.

Or see the summary of everything that ever was, or ever will be, in the silhouette of mountains or the patterns of Orion and Cassiopeia.

There have been many dawns. Mother-of-pearl grays, vermillions, pink ones — laced with gold. Genesis describes how dawns and sunsets separated the days and paved the way for Order. First the salt-water life. Then, as the cycles multiplied, and cellular forms started to show what they could do, the drama took on new proportions. The dinosaurs, and primates.

Whitney came home from nursery school and invited his mother to quiz him on what the class had talked about that day.

"Do you know," he inquired, "what made the dinosaurs disappear?"

"No. What made them disappear?"

"The world changed and they missed the boat!"

The world is always leaving, and the Captain is calling out to us to get aboard.

Then one long blast on the whistle. Up comes the gangplank. It moves out upon the Deep.

Preaching in the morning hours may not guarantee the biggest crowd. But unless we start early it may be too late.

Appendix

Theology And Some Major Concerns

Excerpted from James W. Angell's resume (September 1991 revision)

Theology

My theology is Trinitarian and Reformed.

I believe God is revealed in the natural order of things — in a universe intricately beautiful, adorned with trees, mountains, lakes, light, and the double miracles of life and death. And in Jesus Christ, God made known in history, God in human form, come to redeem, heal, forgive, and make whole. And in the Holy Spirit, "nearer than breathing and closer than hands and feet," who is God as Comforter and Guide. Yet one God, righteous and merciful, striving for us and through us to create a world in which the weak are safe and the strong are just.

I believe in the Bible as a living arena of truth, not a collection of proof texts or dire prophecies about the end of the world.

I believe in the Church as servant, the People of God, called together to continue all that Jesus began to do and teach. I affirm the Great Ends of the Church described in the introductory pages of the Book of Order.

I believe in life after death.

I believe in myself.

I believe in freedom and the integrity of my country in spite of its faults.

I believe in prayer, grace, and love. I believe in my marriage and in the future.

I believe in the Presbyterian Church (U.S.A.), its representative form of government and interdependent structures.

I like the comment of Karl Barth: "Doing theology is like painting a bird in flight." And I like to live on the leading edge of change. I am not satisfied with religious cliches and like to ask what lies behind them in the way of eternal meanings and modern relevance.

I believe in my call to the pastoral and preaching ministry, and feel richly blessed by parents who gave me life, by the various wonderful congregations I have served, by work, my wife and children, health, and the whole adventure of living.

Some Major Concerns (preaching challenges for the 1990s):

Ending the arms race and the threat of nuclear war.

Responding in practical ways to the plight of the homeless and AIDS sufferers.

Finding better answers to substance abuse among persons of all ages, believing that such tragedies often have their roots in the absence of meaningful values and the loss of a love of life and self.

The new challenges of medical ethics and genetic experimentation.

Authentic inclusiveness, our slippage in Civil Rights.

Inclusive language in worship and throughout our structures.

The Independent Living Movement. Maximized living for single and older adults.